CAPTURED
HISTORY

WITHDRAWN

# CIVIL WAR WITNESS

## MATHEW BRADY'S PHOTOS REVEAL THE HORRORS OF WAR

by Don Nardo

Content Adviser: Bob Zeller
Co-Founder and President
The Center for Civil War Photography

COMPASS POINT BOOKS
a capstone imprint

Compass Point Books are published by Capstone,
1710 Roe Crest Drive, North Mankato, Minnesota 56003
www.capstonepub.com

Copyright © 2014 by Compass Point Books, a Capstone imprint.
All rights reserved. No part of this publication may be reproduced in whole or in
part, or stored in a retrieval system, or transmitted in any form or by any means,
electronic, mechanical, photocopying, recording, or otherwise, without written
permission of the publisher.

Managing Editor: Catherine Neitge
Designer: Tracy Davies McCabe
Media Researcher: Wanda Winch
Library Consultant: Kathleen Baxter
Production Specialist: Kathy McColley

Image Credits
CriaImages.com: Jay Robert Nash Collection, 26; Getty Images: George Eastman
House, 23, SSPL, 6, 19; Keya Morgan Collection: LincolnImages.com, 32, 54; Library
of Congress: Prints and Photographs Division, 25, 56, 57 (top), Andrew Russell,
53, James W. Rosenthal, 59 (bottom), John W. Draper, 21, Mathew Brady Galleries,
8, 37, 39, 51, 58 (tl, b), Mathew Brady Galleries/Alexander Gardner, 28, 57 (b),
Mathew Brady Galleries/Mathew Brady, cover, 35, 42, 46 (all), 58 (tr), Mathew Brady
Galleries/Timothy H. O'Sullivan, 30, Timothy H. O'Sullivan, 11, 29, 36 (all), 44;
National Archives and Records Administration (NARA): Mathew Brady Galleries, 5,
13, 14, 17, 41, Mathew Brady Galleries/Mathew Brady, 49, 59 (t); Newscom: Picture
History, 10; U.S. Army Military History Institute, 12; Wikipedia, 18

**Library of Congress Cataloging-in-Publication Data**
Nardo, Don, 1947–
    Civil War witness: Mathew Brady's photos reveal the horrors of war / by Don Nardo.
        pages cm.—(Captured history)
    Includes bibliographical references and index.
    ISBN 978-0-7565-4693-9 (library binding)
    ISBN 978-0-7565-4699-1 (paperback)
    ISBN 978-0-7565-4697-7 (ebook PDF)
1. United States—History—Civil War, 1861–1865—Photography—Juvenile
literature. 2. Brady, Mathew B., ca. 1823–1896—Juvenile literature. 3. War
photographers—United States—History—19th century—Juvenile literature.
4. Photographers—United States—Biography—Juvenile literature. 5. United
States—History—Civil War, 1861–1865—Biography—Juvenile literature. I. Title.
    E468.7.N37 2014
    973.7022'2—dc23                                    2013005348

Printed in the United States of America in North Mankato, Minnesota.
032013      007223CGF13

# TABLEOFCONTENTS

# ChapterOne
# BRADY OF BROADWAY GOES TO WAR

Mathew Brady struggled to guide his horses away from patches of mud in a field near McPherson's Woods. The field was vacant and quiet. But he knew that fewer than two weeks earlier, in the first days of July 1863, it and other places near the village of Gettysburg had been scenes of utter horror. They had been alive with the shudders and shouts of masses of men moving back and forth in a kind of dance of death.

After what some were saying might be a major turning point in the Civil War, many Americans wanted more than written descriptions of the epic battle in eastern Pennsylvania. They craved visual records—photographs of the fields where so many brave men, northerners and southerners alike, had fallen. Brady, as he usually did, aimed to give the public what it wanted as quickly as he could.

It was vital, therefore, to keep his what-is-it wagon from getting bogged down in the mud. He may have recalled, perhaps with a smile, how that quaint name for the mobile darkrooms had come about. At the war's start, there was no particular term for them. Soldiers had quizzed Brady and other photographers about them. They had asked "What is it?" so many times that they soon came to be known as "what-is-it wagons."

Such specially equipped vehicles were a necessity for photographers in the field. In those days, capturing

> Brady, as he usually did, aimed to give the public what it wanted as quickly as he could.

**Mathew Brady posed for his camera operator in a field near Gettysburg's McPherson's Woods.**

subjects outdoors in full daylight required much more than just a camera and a tripod to rest it on. Practical, reliable cameras had existed for only a few years. Large and bulky by today's standards, they used rectangular glass plates that were coated with a wet, sticky mixture of chemicals and cotton.

To take a photo, a photographer first placed a still-wet plate in a plate holder. He attached it to the back of the camera, removed a cover, aimed the lens at the subject, and exposed the plate to the light for several seconds.

A handcart served as a portable darkroom and also carried equipment in the mid 1850s, in the very early days of photography.

To develop the images that had formed on the plates, photographers needed to handle them in completely dark chambers. They coined the term "darkroom" to describe such a chamber.

Keeping the light out was no problem in the specially constructed darkrooms Brady had installed in his photography studios in New York City and Washington, D.C. There, in the years before the war, he had become the most famous and successful photographer in the country. From presidents and generals to ordinary citizens and

From presidents and generals to ordinary citizens and soldiers, people came from far and wide to sit for the great "Brady of Broadway."

soldiers, people came from far and wide to sit for the great "Brady of Broadway," as he had come to be called.

But devising a workable mobile darkroom for taking photos on location was a major challenge. Taking pictures was especially difficult in a war. As troops marched to and fro and furious battles erupted in places near and far, photographers had little or no control over their subjects. Moreover, they had to follow them from place to place, often on a moment's notice. Horse-drawn wagons were the most effective way to carry photography supplies and mobile darkrooms across the countryside. To keep the darkrooms as light-tight as possible, Brady wrapped heavy sheets of canvas around the wagon's wooden walls. But in solving one problem, he had created another. The darkrooms were airtight as well as light-tight. So they became extremely hot inside during the summer. Even worse, they reeked of chemicals, and breathing them caused Brady and his assistants to grow light-headed. While they were developing photos, they had to take breaks and rush outside for fresh air. But during battles the air outside could be just as bad. Instead of chemicals, it reeked of death.

These were only some of the technical obstacles that Brady and other pioneers of photography had to overcome to document the bloody clash between the North and South.

When the American Civil War began in 1861, Brady and some of his competitors leapt into action. Their goal was to create a visual record of the conflict for both the public and

Brady's what-is-it wagon and his camera operators were on hand to take photos near Petersburg, Virginia, site of an extended Civil War battle.

posterity. In fact, Brady was among the first photographers to fully recognize the camera's potential for creating a permanent record of important historical events.

The Battle of Gettysburg was just such an event. Fought between July 1 and 3, 1863, it involved 164,000 soldiers. And the number of casualties was enormous. About 28,000 Confederates were killed, wounded, or missing, while the Union's losses were nearly as bad, at roughly 23,000. The battle was not only huge, but also strategically critical. After boldly invading the North through Pennsylvania, the Confederates had to retreat into their own territory. The South was never again able to mount a major offensive in the North.

Because of the battle's vital importance, Brady and his competitors had known that demand for any photos relating to Gettysburg would be high. So they had gathered their equipment and hurried to the area in hopes of cashing in. First on the scene was one of the more talented photographers of the time—Scottish-born Alexander Gardner. He had worked for Brady for about six years before striking out on his own in 1863. Accompanied by two other former Brady employees—James Gibson and Timothy O'Sullivan—Gardner arrived at Gettysburg around July 5. Brady arrived about July 15.

Brady and Gardner each took several of what came to be seen as classic, even iconic, Civil War photos. In fact, among the thousands of pictures Brady and Gardner took in their careers, the ones they produced at Gettysburg rank among their finest.

Each collection, however, has a distinctive overall look and tone. This is mostly because Gardner and Brady arrived at Gettysburg 10 days apart. Gardner got there just two or three days after the fighting. Some of the corpses of men slain in the battle were still strewn about. So most of the shots by Gardner and his associates were gruesome but dramatic.

Alexander Gardner photographed the Civil War from beginning to end. After the war he headed west to photograph the route of the Union Pacific Railroad.

One of the best known photos shows a group of dead bodies in a wheat field. Another focuses on a dead soldier sprawled between two large boulders in an area known as Devil's Den. Evidence shows that the soldier's body was posed for the picture. Gardner and his associates moved the corpse from its original position 72 yards (66 meters) away and carefully arranged it to produce the greatest artistic and shock value.

Gardner did not acknowledge tampering with historical truth, however. In the photographic sketchbook

Gardner titled the photo taken at Devil's Den on July 6, 1863, "Home of a Rebel Sharpshooter."

he kept during the war, he wrote that he had "found in a lonely place the [hiding place] of a rebel sharpshooter, and photographed the scene presented here. ... The sharpshooter had evidently been wounded in the head by a fragment of shell which had exploded over him, and had laid down upon his blanket to await death. There was no means of judging how long he had lived after receiving his wound, but the disordered clothing shows that his sufferings must have been intense."

Brady (far left), who often inserted himself in his photos to give perspective, took serene pictures at Gettysburg.

This was not a common practice, although some authors have said it was. A scholar of Civil War photography, Bob Zeller, says this was the only known example in the conflict of a photographer moving a body. "Gardner and other photographers," he points out, "sometimes added props, such as muskets, canteens, shells, and such, but with the exception of this corpse, they left the bodies alone."

By the time Brady arrived at Gettysburg, more than a week later, all the bodies that had lain in fields and woods around the village had been buried or removed. So most of the 36 photos he took there are panoramic battlefield

# THE BLOODY CIVIL WAR

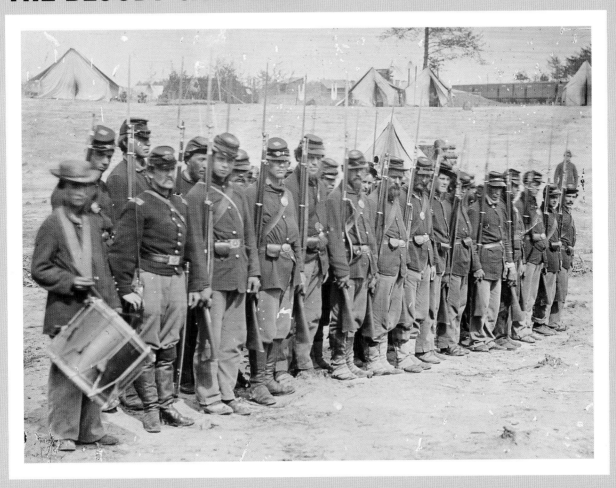

*Brady photographed Maine infantry soldiers after the Second Battle of Fredericksburg in May 1863.*

The great conflict that Mathew Brady photographed in almost painstaking detail—the American Civil War—was one of the most lethal civil wars in history. Fought from 1861 to 1865, it brought more than 3 million people into bloody opposition, mostly over the issue of slavery. The South supported the policy of allowing the practice to expand and thrive. The North was determined to contain slavery's growth.

Nearly every American either fought in the war or knew someone who did. A great many on both sides also knew someone who had lost his or her life in the conflict. The death toll was huge. More than 620,000 soldiers were killed, and as many as 100,000 civilians died. And recent evidence suggests that these staggering figures are too low. More Americans lost their lives in the Civil War than in all other wars combined. About 2.5 percent of the nation's population died in the war. By comparison, 2.5 percent of today's U.S. population is nearly 8 million people.

Another huge casualty, it turned out, was slavery. The North was victorious, and slavery was not simply contained, but eradicated. Like others who risked their lives to preserve images of the conflict, Brady felt that events of such enormous significance had to be recorded. The difference between him and earlier war journalists was that he used a camera rather than a pen.

Brady (right) with Union General Robert B. Potter (fourth from left) and staff in Petersburg, Virginia, in 1864

shots. They show various places where wild charges and blood-spattered clashes had taken place. Sites such as Little Round Top, Culp's Hill, and Cemetery Ridge appear serene in Brady's images. As an expert at the Smithsonian Institution pointed out, in these shots Brady "was striving for an emotional effect that would transcend" the shock of seeing heaps of grisly corpses. "Nearly all of Brady's views of Gettysburg depict significant battle sites as empty landscapes, inviting melancholy speculation without the painful intrusion of shocking detail."

The photos Brady took at Gettysburg, along with others he took during the Civil War, have been labeled iconic or groundbreaking. Yet no Brady photo or group of photos became as iconic as Brady himself. He ended up a living legend, and a legend after his death, for photographing that extraordinary American war almost in its entirety.

More important, Brady's influence on other war photographers of his day was powerful. His earliest photos of the conflict did more than astound and move the American public. They awakened the ambitions and desires of many people who owned or wanted to have the newfangled devices known as cameras.

As Civil War historian Dorothy Kunhardt has pointed out, "Brady's initial success helped inspire hundreds of other photographers to cover future battlefields." For this remarkable achievement, Americans, indeed people everywhere, owe him a debt that can never be repaid.

# Chapter Two

# PHOTOGRAPHY'S PIONEERS

Two days after Mathew Brady died, on January 15, 1896, New York City art dealer Samuel P. Avery honored his memory by sending a message to the *New York Daily Tribune*. The newspaper printed it the next day. Like many other discerning Americans, Avery singled out Brady's single greatest accomplishment—creating an iconic body of artistic work in his renowned collection of Civil War photos.

When the terrible conflict erupted, Avery said, Brady "established himself in Washington, and soon put a corps of [photographers] upon the various fields of action, continuing their services until the close of the war. During those years he gathered over 30,000 negatives, representing many fields of battle, showing the earthworks, the dead, the wounded, the captured prisoners, portraits of famous officers and thousands of scenes and incidents occurring during that eventful epoch ... Mr. Brady is still warmly remembered by many of our old residents, as a most talented and enthusiastic artist, and as a modest, gentle, generous man."

Avery had met Brady in 1839, when they were young men trying to make places for themselves in the emerging New York City artists' community. So Avery knew something about the famous photographer that most Americans did not—that Brady had not been simply

Brady (in center with straw hat near cannon wheel) stands with Union soldiers on Confederate fortifications that were captured at Petersburg in June 1864.

a talented portrait photographer and war chronicler. He also had been one of the pioneers of the photographic art. Fortunate to be in the right place at the right time, he had known and learned from most of the originators of the art.

One of the pioneers of American photography was painter and inventor Samuel F.B. Morse, creator of the telegraph and Morse code. Hoping to drum up interest in that new apparatus, Morse traveled to Europe in 1838. There he learned about an extraordinary device called a camera that could capture the exact image of a person or

object. French artists Joseph-Nicéphore Niépce and Louis Daguerre had worked on the invention together from 1829 to 1833, when Niépce had died, leaving Daguerre to continue their work.

Morse tracked down and met with Daguerre, who showed him his camera. It used a process centered on a thin, rectangular copper plate. The plate was coated with a thin, polished layer of silver and exposed to fumes of

Daguerre's 1838 picture of the Boulevard du Temple in Paris is believed to be the first photograph of living people—a man having his shoes shined (bottom center). The exposure time was too long to capture moving traffic on the street.

**The 1840 equipment used to produce a daguerreotype**

iodine and bromide. The camera operator slipped it into the back of the camera, which was basically an empty box. Sunlight entering a lens in the front of the box traveled to the silver-coated plate and recorded on it an image of whatever was in front of the camera.

Morse was impressed with the invention, calling it "one of the most useful, as well as beautiful, discoveries of the age." When he returned to New York in 1839, he built his own camera based on Daguerre and Niépce's version. Soon Morse was able to produce images called daguerreotypes in honor of Daguerre.

Morse's daguerreotypes may have been the first ever taken in North America. (A few others, including D.W. Seager and Joseph Saxton, were also experimenting with daguerreotypes. No one knows who produced the first one.) One of Morse's early shots showed an 1839 Broadway street scene dominated by the imposing Unitarian Church of the Messiah. Thrilled, Morse predicted the emergence of an entirely new art form, saying in part, "As the bee gathers her sweets for winter, we shall have rich material … an exhaustless store for the imagination to feed on."

Morse soon began working closely with John W. Draper, another photography pioneer. Draper was a chemistry professor and physician who was a founder of what became New York University School of Medicine. Also inspired by Daguerre's work, Draper produced in early 1840 the first known clear image of a woman's face. The portrait was of his sister Dorothy. Another feat credited to Draper is the first detailed photo of the moon, created later that year. In this way, American photography was born in the few months spanning 1839 and 1840.

Young Mathew Brady was fortunate to have arrived in New York City and met both Morse and Draper during these historic months. Brady had grown up on a small farm in the countryside near Lake George, in northern New York. At age 16 he struck out on his own, moving to the nearby town of Saratoga, where he met artist William Page, then in his 20s. They quickly hit it off. Recognizing that Brady too had artistic talent, Page invited him to help out in Page's portrait-painting studio in Albany, New York. In the months that followed, Brady mastered the basics of drawing and learned to paint.

Dorothy Catherine Draper sat still without blinking for more than a minute when her brother photographed her in 1840. He dusted her face with flour to enhance the contrast.

The man who had taught Page to paint was none other than Samuel Morse. Apparently because he wanted to reestablish his relationship with Morse, Page left Albany for New York City in 1839. Brady, who saw a chance to make a name for himself in a big city, went with him.

Not long after their arrival in New York, Page introduced Brady to Morse and Draper. Morse "had just come home from Paris," Brady later recalled, where he had seen "a remarkable discovery one Daguerre, a friend of his, had made in France." Brady called this important innovation an "embryo camera." In 1840 Morse opened the first photography school in the United States, and Brady was among his first students.

Brady's early good fortune was not confined to learning how to use a camera from one of photography's pioneers. In that same crucial period—1839 and 1840—the young man also met one of photography's great commercial innovators, John Plumbe. More than anyone else at the time, Plumbe foresaw that taking portraits with a camera could be much more than a novelty or technical tool. He realized that galleries open to the public could attract a variety of people and become highly profitable.

Plumbe swiftly showed that he was right. Late in 1840 he opened a photography studio in Washington, D.C., and he went on to create the world's first chain of such studios. At the height of his success, he owned branches in Boston, New York, Philadelphia, Baltimore, Louisville, New Orleans, St. Louis, and even in England and France. Brady almost certainly got the idea of building a chain of studios from Plumbe.

Plumbe also made clear that it was not cheap to open a photo gallery. So for almost four years Brady saved the required money by working at odd jobs. These included making small wooden cases for surgical instruments and larger versions to hold finished photographic plates. Exactly where he made the cases is not known. But an 1843 New York City directory mentions his name in connection with a modest business on Fulton Street.

In 1840 Morse opened the first photography school in the United States, and Brady was among his first students.

A lithograph of Mathew Brady appeared in the first edition of *The Photographic Art Journal* in 1851.

In the spring of 1844, when Brady was 21, he opened his first gallery. Called the Daguerrean Miniature Gallery, it was in the "Times Square" of that era—the commercially busy junction of Broadway and Fulton Street. The studio was on the second floor of a redbrick loft building with the prestigious address of 205 Broadway. Brady authority James D. Horan describes other distinctions the young photographer acquired in his first business foray: Brady "hired a carpenter to construct skylights in the roof. He was the first photographer, as far as we know, to use these, which became standard equipment in most studios in later years. ... [W]hen the American Institute held its first competitive photographic exhibition [in 1844], Brady walked off with the silver medal for first honors. ... In the next four years, Brady took the same top prize. In fact, in 1849 it had become so monotonous that *Humphrey's Journal* (one of the early daguerreian trade periodicals) announced with a casual air, 'Mr. B. has won again.'"

Well before 1849, Brady, still in his 20s, had come to be known as "Brady of Broadway." His success came partly from his location, one of the best business sites in the country. But no less important were other factors: his gallery was attractive and comfortable, he hired talented, hard-working people to operate his cameras, and he was a highly skilled artist. He knew how to pose his clients effectively and how to create pictures that were balanced, well-lit, and at times dramatic. As a photography expert of that era commented, "No one can be a successful daguerreotypist unless he is an artist, as well as a manipulator. As a mere rhymer is not a poet, a mere talker not an orator, so a mere manipulator is not capable of producing agreeable pictures, however good his subjects may be. A real artist, with the most unpromising subjects, will surpass him."

These qualities carried through in the other galleries Brady opened in the years that followed. His first Washington, D.C., gallery appeared in 1848. And he

**Mathew Brady's New York gallery**

opened his second New York City studio in 1853. Although he made portraits of anyone who could afford his fees, his sterling reputation particularly attracted the rich and prominent. Among many others, his famous clients included former President Andrew Jackson, future presidents Millard Fillmore and Abraham Lincoln, former first lady Dolley Madison, novelist James Fenimore Cooper, poet Edgar Allan Poe, and Mormon leader Brigham Young.

Among the many less well-known but quite wealthy people who sat for Brady's cameras was a successful

A daguerreotype portrait of Mathew Brady, his wife, Juliette Handy Brady (left), and a Mrs. Haggerty, possibly Juliette's sister

Maryland lawyer named Samuel Handy. While photographing him at the Washington gallery, Brady met Handy's daughter, Juliette Elizabeth, whose family and friends called her Julia. She and Brady fell in love, married, and remained devoted to each other until her death almost 40 years later. Julia took a strong interest in his work and often visited him at his studios.

She also got to know her husband's skilled camera operators and other assistants. Among their number over the years were Austin A. Turner, George S. Cook, Thomas Le Mere, Luther Boswell, Silas Holmes, Timothy O'Sullivan, and James Gibson. Most of them later became independent, quite prominent photographers. The most famous was Alexander Gardner, the Scottish technician Brady hired in 1856. An effective businessman, Gardner not only operated cameras and posed clients, but also helped his boss run the galleries. (For a while, Gardner managed the Washington gallery on his own.)

The two men eventually parted ways. Gardner left Brady's employ in 1863, ready to strike out on his own. Leaving also would allow him to get full credit for the Civil War photos he took. While still on Brady's payroll, Gardner, aided by James Gibson, shot many photos of military camps in the conflict's first year. In 1862 they captured battlefield scenes and the first images of dead soldiers lying as they fell at Antietam in Maryland. Gardner and Gibson copyrighted many of the images, and their names are visible in small print at the bottoms of the photos.

However, these pictures were shown to the public at Brady's galleries and sold with "Brady Album Gallery" labels. Woodcut engravings of the Antietam images published in *Harper's Weekly* were identified as "photographs by Brady." Many people, including some later historians, assumed that Brady himself had taken all of them instead of the actual photographer, who often was unidentified. This was "not an uncommon practice at the time," historian William A. Frassanito points out.

"Most large firms then in the business of photographing scenes for the mass market rarely mentioned the names of individual cameramen."

Gardner understood that this tradition was part of the photography business. But he may have felt that it interfered with his progress toward his own major goal. He wanted to build a reputation for himself as an individual photographer by compiling and selling his own collection of war photos. This and other issues may have made him decide, around the beginning of 1863, to split with Brady.

While still working for Brady, Alexander Gardner took more than 100 battlefield photos following the September 1862 Battle of Antietam. It was the first time an American battlefield had been photographed before the dead were buried.

# WHY NO PHOTOS OF FIGHTING?

*Alfred R. Waud sketched on the battlefield at Gettysburg for* Harper's Weekly.

Although Mathew Brady and other Civil War photographers were often on or near battlefields when the fighting was occurring, they did not succeed in capturing any up-close battle scenes. Only a handful of photos showing distant battle action were taken during the war.

Author John T. Marck explains why: "Brady and his staff photographed the horrors of war, as well as landscapes, battlefields, the glory and horrors of the aftermath of battle, weapons used, and life in the camps, as well as the soldiers themselves. Although it is widely known that battlefield fighting was believed to be photographed, it was difficult to accomplish. ... On the battlefield, people were generally not standing still, thus the image was blurred. Because of this, almost all battlefield action scenes were recorded by artists, who drew pen-and-ink sketches of the action. These completed sketches were then taken from the battlefield and hurried back to various editorial offices where they were turned into wood engravings for printing in such publications as *Leslie's Weekly, Harper's Weekly,* the *New York Illustrated News,* and the *London Illustrated News.*"

Timothy O'Sullivan, who worked for Brady during the early years of the war, photographed Brady's what-is-it wagon at the Second Battle of Bull Run in 1862.

The fact that Brady was given credit or took credit for photos actually taken by his camera operators does not diminish his legacy as a Civil War photographer and chronicler. He paid for the expensive photographic expeditions and personally was in the field during every year of the war. Even in his portrait photography, he had long felt he had a duty to history. "From the first," he recalled in an interview in 1891, shortly before he died, "I regarded myself as under obligation to my country to preserve the faces of its historic men and mothers."

Moreover, he said, his responsibility to posterity went beyond staged, tightly controlled portraits of well-known people. True, for a major photographer like Brady, the war clearly presented an opportunity to increase his fame and make more money. Yet to him, the coming of the conflict represented much more. He also recognized that any pictures he could create of the war would, like his earlier portraits of Jackson, Lincoln, and Poe, live on and benefit future generations.

Therefore, as Brady later recalled, the moment the conflict started he knew he would not be content to sit it out and simply go about his studio business. He immediately began preparing his mobile darkrooms and gathering the equipment he would need to work for long periods in the field. Many of his friends and relatives, including his wife, were alarmed by this sudden flurry of activity. They did not want him to risk his life for the sake of capturing images of violence and dead bodies. But his sense that fate had called him to duty drove him to ignore their objections.

"My wife and my most conservative friends," he later said, "had looked unfavorably upon the departure from commercial business to pictorial war correspondence, and I can only describe the destiny that overruled me by saying that, like Euphorion, [a mythological character who had wings and felt obliged to use them], I felt that I had to go. A spirit in my feet said, 'Go,' and I went."

Brady tried to capture images of the war's first battle— at Bull Run, about 30 miles (48 kilometers) southwest of Washington—in July 1861. The following month *Humphrey's Journal* said he had produced "the only

In a print from the original glass negative, the tip of a sword scabbard peeks from Mathew Brady's coat. The photographer posed for the camera the day after the First Battle of Bull Run.

reliable records" of the engagement and "some of the most curious effects as yet produced in photography." This report seems incorrect, however. Although he was seen on the battlefield with his camera, no evidence exists that Brady returned from Bull Run with any pictures. Most of

> "Brady's name, coupled with his financial backing of other cameramen, resulted in the excellent photographic coverage of the Civil War."

his equipment was damaged during the frenzied retreat of the panic-stricken northern troops.

Brady more than made up for his unsuccessful first try at war photography. In the months that followed, he or his assistants took many photos of battlefields, fallen fighters, encamped soldiers, and important generals and other officers. These became crucial documents of the war. Just as Brady had envisioned, they recorded much of its epic, horrifying scope for later generations. By the time he arrived at Gettysburg in July 1863, he had set the standard for *all* war photographers. In the words of an expert on these men, "Brady, more than any other person, with the possible exception of Gardner, was *the* prime factor in the establishment of this corps of Civil War photographers. Brady's name, coupled with his financial backing of other cameramen, resulted in the excellent photographic coverage of the Civil War."

It is vital to emphasize that Brady was well aware of, and likely quite proud of, his pivotal role as a sort of godfather of war photographers. As he and his assistants unpacked their equipment and prepared to capture images of the Gettysburg battlefields, he almost surely felt that fate had drawn him there. And as he composed his shots, a moving realization must have repeatedly occurred to him: He was creating something for all time, and most of those who would gaze on these pictures were not yet born.

# Chapter Three

# ICONIC LANDMARKS AND LEADERS

Mathew Brady is most famous for his Civil War photos. Many of them captured the locales and landmarks where battles, troop movements, and other historic events took place. Other images produced by Brady's cameras showed President Abraham Lincoln, generals and other officers, and other notable leaders of the conflict.

It is impractical, if not impossible, to select a single Brady war photo that stands out from all the others. Would it be his famous photograph of Robert E. Lee at the back door of his home in Richmond, which was taken by Brady just days after Lee's surrender? Is it his striking image of three Rebel prisoners at Gettysburg, or citizen-hero John Burns recovering from his battle wounds after joining the fight with the Union boys? There are simply too many that fit the definitions of iconic, historic, classic, or highly memorable.

This is partly because Brady was a gifted artist who happened to be even better with a camera than he was with paints and brushes. As a result, a great many of his pictures were and remain not only slices of history, but also minor artistic masterpieces. Moreover, the ability to combine the roles of historian and artist came naturally to him, and he did not know how to be one and not the other. As Mary Panzer, formerly with the Smithsonian National Portrait Gallery, said, "Brady saw no need to

> It is impractical, if not impossible, to select a single Brady war photo that stands out from all the others.

Abraham Lincoln credited Brady's 1860 portrait with helping him win the presidential election that year.

# THE OLD HERO OF GETTYSBURG

*Brady photographed John L. Burns and was then photographed himself seated near the back of the house (at right).*

In a departure from his wide battlefield images, Mathew Brady took three photos of John L. Burns, sometimes called the "old hero of Gettysburg." A veteran of the War of 1812, Burns was 70 years old when the North and South clashed in the fields surrounding the usually quiet village of Gettysburg, where he lived. On July 1, 1863, he heard the sounds of guns firing in the distance. When he found out what was happening, he grabbed his old-fashioned flintlock musket and headed out to fight alongside the federal troops.

Burns soon met a wounded Union soldier. The soldier agreed to lend his more advanced musket to the older man, who fearlessly entered the fray. Burns distinguished himself as a sharpshooter, even managing to shoot a southern officer off his charging horse. Wounded several times, the old man dragged himself to safety. His story appeared in many northern newspapers. For a while he was a kind of national hero. That explains why Brady felt it was important to include shots of him in his Gettysburg collection.

Two of the pictures show Burns sitting proudly in a rocking chair outside the basement of his white clapboard house. The crutches he was using while recuperating from his wounds can be seen behind him. To his left, his flintlock leans against the door.

The third photo in the set is a view of the entire house from across the street. Burns and his wife are visible on a small porch with stairs leading to the ground. For a long time following the war, and even well after Brady's death, no one noticed a tiny background detail in this photo. It was not until 2001 that the Library of Congress started making high-resolution digital scans of many of Brady's original negatives. This allowed researchers to see details that had been almost invisible before. In 2004, while examining the background of the photo of Burns' house, a researcher noticed Brady, wearing his customary straw hat, sitting on a second stairway near the back of the house.

Also visible in the background of the digital blowup is Brady's portable developing tent. That clever device consisted of a tripod holding up a wooden box that was wrapped with a large piece of dark cloth to keep out the light. A photographer or assistant standing under the cloth would put his head and arms into the box to prepare the next plate for the camera.

**The view from Seminary Ridge was one of Brady's many photographs taken at Gettysburg.**

separate truth from art." He sought to create an "ideal," a visually balanced and beautiful "historical territory for the American people, and he was successful."

One way to attempt the difficult job of singling out some of Brady's best war-related work is to examine a series or collection of images having a central unifying theme. Of his many collections showing physical landmarks, the series of shots he took at Gettysburg in mid-July 1863 is among the more artistically memorable and historically important. And among the hundreds of portraits he took of war leaders, probably none are more iconic than those of Ulysses S. Grant and Robert E. Lee, the two most renowned generals of the conflict.

Examining Brady's Gettysburg photos first, evidence shows that two of his assistants, David B. Woodbury and Anthony Berger, arrived in the village a couple of days before their boss did. Apparently Brady was held up by travel restrictions connected with military turmoil in southern Pennsylvania. While waiting for him, Berger and Woodbury unexpectedly encountered Gardner and his own assistants, who were just leaving the area. Gardner likely explained that all of the bodies of the fallen had recently been buried. Brady would not be able to capture the butchery and carnage that so graphically reflected the human tragedy that had occurred in the fields surrounding Gettysburg.

When Brady finally arrived and joined Woodbury and Berger on July 15, therefore, he had to devise a different strategy. The approach he decided on was to show the public what the places and landmarks they had read so much about in the news looked like. For instance, written reports of the fighting had mentioned a central Union defensive point called Culp's Hill. The average person must have tried to imagine what it looked like.

People also probably tried to visualize Little Round Top. During the Gettysburg battle, thousands of Confederate soldiers had died there in a brave but unsuccessful charge against stalwart northern ranks. In a sense, Brady transported his public to Little Round Top and other key places where fighting took place. He tried to provide an illustrated survey of the battle's chief settings.

> The approach he decided on was to show the public what the places and landmarks they had read so much about in the news looked like.

**Brady photographed the battered trees atop Culp's Hill.**

Some of his photos acquired extra theatrical flair by showing physical damage caused by the fighting.

Prominent examples of such damage were plainly visible atop Culp's Hill. Massive barrages of Confederate artillery and muskets had horribly scarred a large number of trees. Some of their tops had been completely blasted off. After scaling the hill and marveling at what they found, Brady and his companions took four pictures. These shots later helped to attract tourists to the spot.

In fact, in the months and years after the battle, Culp's Hill became far and away the most popular destination for visitors to the Gettysburg region. It took 20 or more years for nature to heal or replace the disfigured trees and reclaim the area.

Another battlefield scene captured in multiple images was of a wheat field near a large stand of trees known as McPherson's Woods. Somewhere in the woods on the battle's first day a Confederate sharpshooter had killed Union General John F. Reynolds. A very popular military leader, Reynolds was widely seen by northerners as one of the best, if not *the* best, general the Union had. So the public had a strong interest in seeing where he fell. In one of the shots, McPherson's Woods looms in the distance at the upper right. In the field in the foreground are two men. The one on the left points out the woods to the other, who is none other than Brady himself, wearing his signature straw hat.

In fact, the famous photographer appears in at least six of the photos his cameramen took at Gettysburg. One reason seems to have been Brady's interest in providing perspective. His expert eye told him that the absence of the dead bodies that had dominated most of Gardner's images presented a possible problem. Without corpses, or perhaps a horse or a house, Brady evidently thought, the size of objects and the distances in some of the pastoral panoramas would not be readily apparent to the city folk who were most of his customers.

**Brady (far right), standing in the field near McPherson's Woods, provides perspective to the photo's viewer.**

To add a familiar object for comparison, therefore, Brady inserted himself into some of the shots. An especially striking example is another of the photos of McPherson's Woods. At first it appears to be a charming scene showing the photographer standing beside a rail fence bordering a small stream. He stares away from the camera across a deserted field toward the woods. There, it was thought, General Reynolds had been killed.

Most of the scenes in Brady's photos at Gettysburg are not only deserted, but also observed from a distance.

Three Confederate prisoners pose for Brady's camera following the Union victory at Gettysburg.

Besides some of the well-known spots where fighting had occurred, the photos include several views of the village of Gettysburg seen from afar and from different directions. By design, these distant panoramas lack much in the way of detail.

In a few notable changes of pace, however, Brady deliberately and deftly captured some subjects in considerable detail. In creating one of his most famous and most popular Gettysburg photos, he posed three Confederate prisoners atop a pile of rails on Seminary

Ridge, just west of the village. Who these men were and where they had come from remain unknown. Perhaps Brady and his assistants encountered a Union patrol taking the captives somewhere. If so, they may have asked the guards to let the prisoners briefly pose for a picture. In that case, we must assume that the guards, holding their weapons, were standing behind the camera throughout the session.

The captives must have enjoyed this diversion. Brady posed them in, or at least allowed them to assume, stances that displayed their pride as soldiers. Some observers have seen in their body language a touch of defiance for the enemy. The prisoners' uniforms and equipment are visible in great detail. This was very helpful to later historians, filmmakers, Civil War re-enactors, and others interested in accurately reconstructing what soldiers wore and carried in that period.

At first glance, one might suppose that Gardner's Gettysburg photos had trumped Brady's. After all, Gardner created many detailed, at times striking, shots of the dead. With the single exception of the posed corpse in Devil's Den, the bodies lay in or near the spots where they had fallen during the momentous battle. So Gardner likely was confident that his dramatically gruesome images would capture the public's interest more than Brady's. After all, most of Brady's pictures depicted empty scenes. While at Gettysburg, Gardner wrote in his sketchbook: "The distorted dead recall the ancient legends of men

**Who these men were and where they had come from remain unknown.**

A Gettysburg photo that appeared in Gardner's *Photographic Sketchbook of the Civil War* was titled "A Harvest of Death."

torn in pieces by the savage [immorality] of fiends. Swept down without preparation, the shattered bodies fall in all conceivable positions. ... Such a picture conveys a useful moral: It shows the blank horror and reality of war, in opposition to its pageantry. Here are the dreadful details! Let them aid in preventing such another calamity falling upon the nation."

As it turned out however, it was Brady who trumped Gardner. Perhaps because Brady proved a better marketer, in August 1863 the widely read *Harper's Weekly* ignored Gardner's efforts and published woodcut engravings of 11

Gardner "had scooped Brady in the fields, but Brady, the master of promotion, had scooped Gardner in the press."

of Brady's photos. As scholar Bob Zeller says, "Gardner, working apart from Brady, had beaten his old boss to the battlefield and captured the only photographs of the dead at Gettysburg. He had scooped Brady in the fields, but Brady, the master of promotion, had scooped Gardner in the press. When the thousands of readers opened their *Harper's Weekly* to see the graphic coverage at Gettysburg, from photographs converted into woodcut engravings, once again the credit line they saw was 'Photographs by Brady.'"

Brady used another tactic to promote himself and his galleries even as he continued his earnest attempt to document the war for posterity. An effective way to achieve both, he concluded, was to create detailed portraits of the conflict's leaders. It was a longtime habit of his; he had been taking photos of prominent Americans since the 1840s. Particularly fascinating to the public were field generals like Grant and Lee. The press thrilled readers with its written descriptions of the exploits of these larger-than-life characters. But the average person knew little of a personal nature about them, including what they looked like.

Brady's portraits of the generals were, therefore, a kind of public service. They provided a way for people to see such living legends up close, to look them in the eye, so to speak, and get a glimpse of their humanity. During the war a *New York Times* reporter aptly summed up Brady's achievement. The foremost military chiefs on both sides,

General Ulysses S. Grant in the field and in Brady's studio

he said, "are as brilliant but as distant from us as planets; it is a pleasure to have these planets photographed, and be upon whispering terms with the Generals who are now to the nation [seen] as gods."

Brady took pictures of one of these gods—Grant— several times during the final year of the war. In part this was because in mid-1864 Grant chose Brady as the official photographer for the Union's military headquarters at City Point (now Hopewell), Virginia. Grant seems to have extended this honor because his first meeting and sitting with Brady had gone so well, despite a near disaster.

"Brady's camera caught the fatigue, the anxiety and the terrible responsibility that lay upon [Grant's] shoulders."

That historic sitting had taken place a few months before. Early in March 1864, Grant had learned that President Lincoln had decided to give him control of all the northern armies. Five days later Grant had arrived at Brady's Washington gallery to sit for his first official portrait as the Union's supreme commander. The general was accompanied by the secretary of war, Edwin Stanton.

As Stanton quietly watched, Brady posed Grant for a series of shots. Most modern experts view them as among the finest taken of any Civil War general. Grant wore his formal uniform. On each shoulder was the prestigious three-star insignia just awarded him by President Lincoln. (He was the first three-star general since George Washington.) But it is Grant's somber, somewhat haggard look that stands out in these images. In the words of modern Brady authority James D. Horan, "Brady's camera caught the fatigue, the anxiety and the terrible responsibility that lay upon [Grant's] shoulders."

Something else nearly ended up on Grant's shoulders that day, namely shards of flying glass. At one point during the session, Brady felt that the light was too dim. He asked an assistant to move a shade blocking a glass skylight. When the man reached the skylight, he lost his balance and his feet broke through the glass, sending sharp pieces showering down around Grant.

At first horrified, Brady was relieved to see that the general was unhurt. "It was a miracle that some of the pieces didn't strike him," the photographer later recalled.

"And if one had, it would have been the end of Grant; for that glass was two inches thick." Even more astonishing to Brady was Grant's reaction. As the glass rained down, the general remained still, giving the falling shards only a casual glance. It was "the most remarkable display of nerve I ever witnessed," Brady stated.

Most of the war leaders who sat for Brady were, like Grant, northerners. This is not surprising, considering that the photographer was a northerner himself, so he had no access to southern officers while the conflict raged. But Brady bided his time. And very soon after the Confederacy was defeated—a mere 11 days afterward, in fact—he managed to hold a picture-taking session with the South's equivalent of Grant—General Robert E. Lee.

Brady probably reasoned that he had a good chance of getting Lee to sit for him, because the two had met 20 years before. Then a dashing young officer in the U.S. Army, Lee had gone to Brady's New York studio. There Brady had captured his likeness by a camera—what was to him a novel device.

Hoping Lee would remember, Brady boldly went to the general's house in Richmond, Virginia, on April 19, 1865, and knocked on the door. Lee did recall Brady. And after lengthy consideration, and hearing the advice of his wife and a trusted friend, Lee agreed to let Brady photograph him the next day. Wearing his impressive gray formal uniform, the general posed outside the back door of his house. In some shots he stood, while in others he sat in

As the glass rained down, the general remained still, giving the falling shards only a casual glance. It was "the most remarkable display of nerve I ever witnessed."

**Confederate General Robert E. Lee posed for Brady's camera below the back porch of his Richmond house.**

an elegant armchair. Photography scholar Zeller rightly calls these images "among the greatest photographs of the Civil War." Like few photos in history, they attest to the greatness of both the person in front of the camera and the one behind it.

# ChapterFour
# A MASTER OF THE EYE OF HISTORY

When the Civil War ended in 1865, Mathew Brady was only in his early 40s. Still the most famous photographer in the United States, he fully expected to have a long and illustrious career. But as it turned out, his best days, for the most part, were behind him. Once one of the most popular and successful businessmen in the country, he would end up poor, ill, and miserable.

One reason for Brady's downward path was the rapidly changing nature of the photography business. Each year hundreds of young, talented, and ambitious photographers appeared on the scene. Competition within the profession became increasingly fierce.

Also, at his height of success, Brady owned several elegantly decorated studios and employed many camera operators and other assistants. This made his business very expensive to run. By itself, this may not have been a problem. But during the war Brady sank huge amounts of money into extra equipment and personnel to make the thousands of negatives that captured the conflict. (Each negative could be used to produce many positive prints, commonly called photos.) All along he had assumed that his collection, constituting an important visual record of American history, would prove to be tremendously valuable. He had expected to make back the money he had spent to compile it, plus much more, soon after the conflict.

Once one of the most popular and successful businessmen in the country, he would end up poor, ill, and miserable.

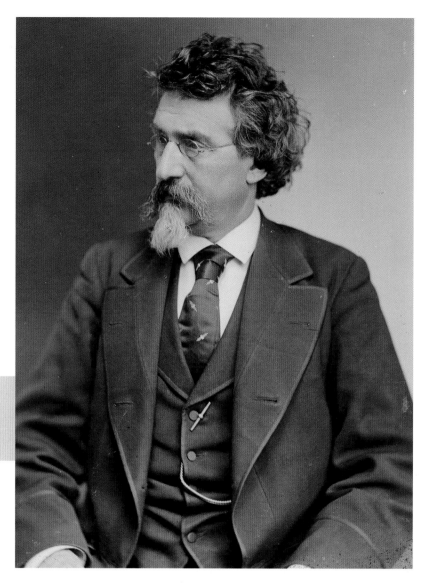

Mathew Brady, about 10 years after the war's end

Unfortunately for Brady, such expectations were little more than pipe dreams. The truth was that, although he was a brilliant and artistic photographer, he was not a very good accountant. In Zeller's words, "His ambition and imagination always seems to exceed his business sense; he spent more than he took in. This was particularly true during the war."

When Brady tried to sell his collection of war negatives to the New York Historical Society in 1866, to his surprise the organization said no. Finding himself falling increasingly into debt, the photographer tried again to sell the collection in 1869. This time the potential buyer was the U.S. Congress.

Brady was certain that the federal government would want to own a permanent visual record of the Civil War, but once more he encountered resistance. Year after year, the national legislators considered obtaining the collection but did not provide the money to buy it. Finally, in 1875 Congress agreed to purchase Brady's war negatives, his single greatest legacy to posterity. But the amount it paid—$25,000—was not nearly enough to erase his enormous debts and keep his last surviving gallery running.

After Congress bought Brady's war negatives they were stored in the U.S. War Department Library. (Other Brady negatives existed in a few other, separate collections of Civil War photographs.) Decades later, in 1940, the National Archives acquired the approximately 6,000 negatives from the War Department.

By that time, however, some of these items were not Brady's. Over the years, more than 1,000 negatives created by Andrew J. Russell, George Barnard, and other lesser known Civil War photographers had made their way into the collection. Most people did not realize that fact. There was a general assumption that all of the negatives were Brady's. So they were routinely referred to, variously, as

A print of a photograph by Andrew Russell of Confederate soldiers killed at the Second Battle of Fredericksburg is one of thousands of Civil War images held by the Library of Congress.

the Brady negatives, the Brady photographs, or the Brady collection. The result, as Bob Zeller points out, was that the "mischaracterization of his role and influence in Civil War photography grew." Put simply, many pictures taken by others came to be credited to Brady.

Yet the importance of Brady's contribution to war photography cannot be overstated. His collection of Civil War images was the first large-scale photographic record of any war. Moreover, Brady was among the first people practicing the new craft and art form of photography to

# BRADY'S SAD DECLINE

*Mathew Brady in a print from the original 1889 glass negative*

Mathew Brady's exploits as a Civil War photographer marked the high point of his career and his life. In the years after the war, he lost all but one of his galleries because of financial problems. He and his wife moved from the first-class hotel they had long lived in to one rundown boarding house after another, until they finally were forced to live in the gallery.

Complicating the situation was a steady decline in Brady's health. His eyesight deteriorated, requiring him to wear glasses with thick, blue-tinted lenses, and he suffered from painful arthritis. Another downward turn occurred in 1881, when one of his employees sued him for unpaid salary and a judge ordered Brady to sell his last gallery to pay the debt.

Meanwhile, Julia Brady's worsening heart condition eventually made her bedridden. After she died, in 1887, Brady started drinking heavily and had to move in with his nephew. As if this were not enough misfortune for one person, in 1895, at age 72, he was hit by a horse-drawn carriage. He made a partial recovery, but it became too hard for his nephew to continue caring for him. So Brady reluctantly allowed some former Civil War soldiers to rent a small apartment for him in New York City. He did not live there long. Late in 1895 he developed a life-threatening kidney condition. He died, almost unnoticed by the public, in a New York hospital on January 15, 1896.

realize that it could be used to preserve historical events. "The camera is the eye of history," he reportedly said. Today he is widely viewed as one of the early masters of that seemingly magical eye.

Brady also was the strongest driving force in ensuring that the American Civil War was properly recorded by cameras. True, other men, including Alexander Gardner, recognized the importance of photographing the war, and they did so with distinction. But it was Brady who had initially hired, trained, and inspired many of these men. And he remained the man to beat, so to speak, in the new area of wartime photographic journalism throughout the conflict. According to historian William Frassanito, Brady's "organizational and leadership abilities, along with his financial backing," were indispensable. Without Brady's contributions, "it is doubtful that the war would have been covered as extensively as it was."

So even if no single iconic Civil War photo emerged to overshadow all the others, one iconic Civil War photographer *did* come to the fore. His name was Mathew Brady. Two major ambitions drove him—the first of which was to become a successful businessman. He accomplished that, admirably, for a brief while. His larger ambition was to visually document his era and a dreadful war for future generations. He achieved that, too, in magnificent fashion, and will be remembered for it for as long as the photographic art survives.

Without Brady's contributions, "it is doubtful that the war would have been covered as extensively as it was."

# Timeline

## c. 1823

Mathew Brady is born in a small town in northern New York

## 1829

French inventors Louis Daguerre (above) and Joseph-Nicéphore Niépce begin working together to perfect a new invention—the camera

## 1848

Brady opens his first photo studio in Washington, D.C.

## 1856

Brady hires Scottish photographer Alexander Gardner

**1839**

Brady goes to New York and meets inventor Samuel Morse (above), who has recently constructed a camera based on one created by Daguerre and Niépce

**1840**

American inventor John Plumbe opens the first of his many photo galleries

**1861**

The Civil War begins; Brady takes camera equipment and mobile darkrooms into the field in hope of photographing the conflict

**1862**

Brady's employees photograph the Peninsula Campaign, the Bull Run battlefield, and the aftermath of Antietam (above); Brady visits Harper's Ferry to photograph troops and joins Union generals George McClellan and Ambrose Burnside on the march as they leave Maryland and invade Virginia in November

# Timeline

## 1863

Gardner leaves Brady's employ and opens his own Washington Gallery; both Brady and Gardner go to Gettysburg, Pennsylvania, and photograph the aftermath of the momentous battle that had recently occurred there

## 1864

Brady is chosen as official photographer for the Union's military headquarters at City Point, Virginia, and takes portraits in the field at Cold Harbor, Virginia, of Grant and other top Union commanders

## 1869

Brady first approaches the U.S. Congress with his war collection but makes no headway

## 1875

Congress finally agrees to buy several thousand of Brady's negatives for $25,000

**1865**

Just 11 days after the South's surrender, ending the war, Brady photographs Confederate General Robert E. Lee in Richmond

**1866**

Brady tries to sell his collection of Civil War negatives to the New York Historical Society, which refuses to buy them

**1896**

Brady dies in a New York hospital; he is buried in Congressional Cemetery in Washington, D.C.

**1940**

The National Archives acquires the Brady negatives bought by Congress in 1875

# Glossary

**artillery:** cannons and other large guns designed to strike an enemy from a distance

**daguerreotype** (dag-EAR-oh-type)**:** early photographic process in which an image is produced on a silver-coated copper plate

**engraving:** an image produced from a drawing or photo that has been carved or otherwise transferred onto wood or metal

**federal:** having to do with the national government in Washington, D.C.

**flintlock:** an early firearm in which a piece of flint struck a piece of steel, producing a spark that ignited gunpowder; the small explosion pushed a bullet forward and out of the gun

**iconic:** memorable or instantly recognizable for having captured the very essence of a person or thing

**melancholy:** sad and thoughtful

**negatives:** photographic images; areas that are light in the original subject are dark in a negative and those that are dark are light; prints can be made from negatives

**panorama:** a very wide, sweeping view or scene

**pastoral:** having to do with the countryside

**posterity:** future ages and generations

**prestigious:** held in high regard

**re-enactors:** modern history buffs who enjoy accurately staging battles and other events from the past

**transcend:** to rise above

**trump:** to outdo or overshadow

# Additional Resources

## Further Reading

Donlan, Leni. *Mathew Brady: Photographing the Civil War.*
Chicago: Raintree, 2008.

DK Publishing. *The Civil War: A Visual History.*
New York: DK Pub., 2011.

Nardo, Don. *Bull Run to Gettysburg: Early Battles of the Civil War.*
Mankato, Minn.: Compass Point Books, 2011.

Stille, Darlene R. *The Civil War Through Photography.*
Chicago: Heinemann Library, 2012.

## Internet Sites

Use FactHound to find Internet sites related
to this book. All of the sites on FactHound
have been researched by our staff.

Here's all you do:
Visit *www.facthound.com*
Type in this code: 9780756546939

## Critical Thinking Using the Common Core

Consider the differences in look and tone in the photographs taken by Mathew Brady and Alexander Gardner after the Battle of Gettysburg. What do you think each photographer was trying to achieve? (Integration of Knowledge and Ideas)

The photo on page 28 shows dead soldiers lying on the ground after the 1862 Battle of Antietam. How does this differ from earlier photos of battlegrounds? (Key Ideas and Details)

What did Mathew Brady mean when he said "The camera is the eye of history"? (Integration of Knowledge and Ideas)

# Source Notes

Page 4, line 22: Bob Zeller. *The Blue and Gray in Black and White: A History of Civil War Photography.* London: Praeger, 2005, p. 75.

Page 11, line 1: Alexander Gardner. *Gardner's Photographic Sketch Book of the Civil War.* New York: Dover, 1959, in text opposite Plate 41.

Page 12, line 5: *The Blue and Gray in Black and White,* p. 107.

Page 14, line 5: "Mathew Brady Gallery, New York. McPherson's Woods at Gettysburg." Smithsonian National Portrait Gallery. 1 March 2013. http://www.npg.si.edu/exh/brady/gallery/59gal.html

Page 15, line 14: Dorothy M. Kunhardt and Philip B. Kunhardt Jr. *Mathew Brady and His World.* Alexandria, Va.: Time-Life Books, 1977, p. 200.

Page 16, line 10: Mary Panzer. *Mathew Brady and the Image of History.* Washington, D.C.: Smithsonian Institution Press, 1997, p. 226.

Page 19, line 7: "Morse reminiscence." *The Philadelphia Photographer* (Vol. IX, No. 97, pp. 1-4.) January 1872. 1 March 2013. The Daguerreian Society. http://www.daguerre.org/resource/texts/morse.html

Page 20, line 5: Merry A. Foresta. "Photos for All Time." *Smithsonian* magazine. April 2004. 1 March 2013. http://www.smithsonianmag.com/arts-culture/photos-for-all-time.html

Page 21, line 7: James D. Horan. *Mathew Brady: Historian With a Camera.* Charleston, S.C.: Nabu Press, 2011, p. 6.

Page 22, line 2: George Alfred Townsend. "Still Taking Pictures: Brady, the Grand Old Man of American Photography." The World. April 1891. 1 March 2013. Helios: Online Collections. http://americanart.si.edu/exhibitions/online/helios/secrets/darkchamber-noframe.html?/exhibitions/online/helios/secrets/text_brady.html

Page 23, line 9: *Mathew Brady: Historian With a Camera,* p. 9.

Page 24, line 19: *Mathew Brady and the Image of History,* p. 47.

Page 27, line 27: William A. Frassanito. *Antietam: The Photographic Legacy of America's Bloodiest Day.* New York: Scribner, 1978, p. 54.

Page 29, line 7: John T. Marck. "Mathew Brady and Photography During the Civil War." 1 March 2013. http://www.aboutfamouspeople.com/article1043.html

Page 30, line 7: "Still Taking Pictures: Brady, the Grand Old Man of American Photography."

Page 31, line 18: Ibid.

Page 31, line 28: *The Blue and Gray in Black and White,* p. 60.

Page 33, line 12: D. Mark Katz. *Witness to an Era: The Life and Photographs of Alexander Gardner: the Civil War, Lincoln, and the West.* New York: Viking, 1991, p. 47.

Page 34, line 25: *Mathew Brady and the Image of History,* p. 120.

Page 43, line 28: *Gardner's Photographic Sketch Book of the Civil War,* in text opposite Plate 36.

Page 45, line 1: *The Blue and Gray in Black and White,* pp. 111–112.

Page 46, line 1: "Photographic Phases." *The New York Times.* 21 July 1862. 4 March 2013. http://www.nytimes.com/1862/07/21/news/photographic-phases.html?scp=4&sq=photography&st=p

Page 47, line 16: *Mathew Brady: Historian With a Camera,* picture 258.

Page 47, line 27: Shelby Foote. *The Civil War A Narrative: Red River to Appomattox.* New York: Random House, 1974, pp. 8-9.

Page 49, line 2: *The Blue and Gray in Black and White,* p. 167.

Page 51, line 4: Email interview with Bob Zeller. 2 Jan. 2013.

Page 53, line 3: *The Blue and Gray in Black and White,* p. 191.

Page 55, line 2: *Mathew Brady: Historian With a Camera,* p. 90

Page 55, line 14: *Antietam: The Photographic Legacy of America's Bloodiest Day,* p. 54.

# Select Bibliography

"Alexander Gardner, Photographer." Civil War Trust. 28 Feb. 2013. http://www.civilwar.org/education/history/biographies/alexander-gardner.html

Burns, Stanley B. *Shooting Soldiers: Civil War Medical Photography By R.B. Bontecou.* New York: Burns Archive, 2011.

Butterfield, Roger. "The Camera Comes to the White House." *American Heritage.* August 1964. 28 Feb. 2013. http://www.americanheritage.com/content/camera-comes-white-house

"Civil War Photographers." American Experience. 28 Feb. 2013. http://www.pbs.org/wgbh/amex/lincolns/atwar/es_camera.html

Frassanito, William A. *Antietam: The Photographic Legacy of America's Bloodiest Day.* New York: Scribner, 1978.

Frassanito, William A. *Early Photography at Gettysburg.* Gettysburg, Pa: Thomas Publications, 1995.

Frassanito, William A. *Grant and Lee: The Virginia Campaigns,* 1864-1865. New York: Scribner, 1983.

Gardner, Alexander. *Gardner's Photographic Sketch Book of the Civil War.* New York: Dover Publications, 1959.

Hogge, Dennis. *Mathew Brady's Manassas Photo Journal: Exploring the First Battlefield of the American Civil War in Period Images.* Centreville, Va.: Old Dominion Publishers, 2011.

Horan, James D. *Mathew Brady: Historian With a Camera.* Charleston, S.C.: Nabu Press, 2011.

Hyslop, Stephen G. *Eyewitness to the Civil War: The Complete History from Secession to Reconstruction.* Washington, D.C.: National Geographic, 2006.

Kagan, Neil. *Great Photographs of the Civil War.* Birmingham, Ala.: Oxmoor House, 2003.

Katz, D. Mark. *Witness to an Era: The Life and Photographs of Alexander Gardner: the Civil War, Lincoln, and the West.* New York: Viking, 1991.

Keya Morgan Collection. "Mathew Brady." 28 Feb. 2013. http://www.mathewbrady.com/

Kunhardt, Dorothy M., and Philip B. Kunhardt Jr. *Mathew Brady and His World.* Alexandria, Va.: Time-Life Books, 1977.

McPherson, James M. *Battle Cry of Freedom: The Civil War Era.* New York: Oxford University Press, 1988.

National Archives. "The Civil War as Photographed by Mathew Brady." 28 Feb. 2013. http://www.archives.gov/education/lessons/brady-photos/

National Portrait Gallery. "Mathew Brady's World: Brady and the Civil War." 28 Feb. 2013. http://www.npg.si.edu/exh/brady/war/civilpg.htm

Panzer, Mary. *Mathew Brady and the Image of History.* Washington, D.C.: Smithsonian Institution Press, 1997.

"Photography and the Civil War." Civil War Trust. 28 Feb. 2013. http://www.civilwar.org/photos/3d-photography-special/photography-and-the-civil-war.html

Russell, Andrew J. *Russell's Civil War Photographs:116 Historic Prints.* New York: Dover Publications, 1982.

Zeller, Bob. *The Blue and Gray in Black and White: A History of Civil War Photography.* Westport, Conn.: Praeger, 2005.

# Index

## About the Author

Historian and award-winning author Don Nardo has written many books for young people about American history. Nardo lives with his wife, Christine, in Massachusetts.